Contents:

It is suggested that once you have revised a topic and are familiar with it you can tick it off.

Materials

Forming techniques

Electronics theory

Coursework guidance

Health & Safety

PPE – Personal Protective Equipment, like hairnets or safety glasses.

Risk assessments – This is a document that tries to identify potential problems and suggest ways to make them less likely to cause harm.

COSHH – Control of Substances Hazardous to Health, this is like a guide of how to use dangerous chemicals or materials and what to do if they get in your eyes etc.

Health and safety of staff is the number one priority to manufacturers. If staff have accidents when using manufacturing equipment it could lead to serious injury or death. To ensure that this does not happen manufacturing companies must:-

1. Produce a production plan that contains information about health and safety,
2. Carry out staff checks, to make sure all staff are trained to use tools and machines,
3. Ensure that *PPE* items are available for all staff to use.
4. Ensure that machines have been checked by a qualified member of staff or engineer certifying they are safe to use.
5. Ensure that all materials and chemicals used have a *COSHH* system in place, and all staff are aware of it.
6. *Risk assessments* are completed for all processes/tasks that staff carry out.

Manufacturing Sectors

For the exam it is important that you know the 9 main manufacturing sectors and you should be able to identify different products made in each sector. These are:

	Manufacturing sectors	Examples of products made in sector
1	Clothing and Textiles	Jeans, trousers, T-shirts, shirts, coats etc
2	Electrical and communications	Blender, TV, Mobile phone, laptop etc
3	Food and Drink	Burger, chips, frozen food, coke etc
4	Furniture	Kitchen table, TV stand, bed, chair etc
5	Machinery and equipment	Pillar drill, pliers, grinder, knife etc
6	Motor manufacturing	Car body, car door, seat belt, engine etc
7	Paper and print	Newspaper, posters, menu, cards etc
8	Chemical and pharmaceutical	Lipstick, antibiotics, bleach, perfume etc
9	Packaging	perfume box, food wrapper, DVD case etc

Stages of Production

There are 5 main stages of production

1) **Material preparation** – Raw materials usually need some preparation before they are able to be used, such as potatoes need washing and peeling, fabric's need washing and colouring, wood needs drying out etc.

2) **Processing** – This is when the raw material is changed some how such as baking, cutting, shaping or mixing etc.

3) **Assembly** – This is when the separate components of the product are joined together usually with glue, welding or fastening.

4) **Finishing** – Takes place after the manufacturing process to give the product its final look, help protect the product against the environment and, make the product safer.

5) **Packaging** – packaging can be used to protect the product from the environment and vice-versa, help make the product look better, make the product easy to store and, provide security so parts don't get lost or damaged.

Packaging can be in the form of boxes, cartons, blister packaging, packets, bottles, drums, cans, vacuum formed plastic cases, pressed card etc.

Quality control

Companies need to get a balance of making a product as fast as possible but at a suitable standard as the faster they can make a product at a reasonable standard the less it costs them. But as the speed increases it is easier to make mistakes in the production, if these mistakes are not spotted it can cost the company much more money later in unhappy customers and refunds. So quality checks are put in place to ensure that the product is made to an acceptable standard.

First companies must decide what to check, when to check it and how. They also need to teach their staff the procedure for carrying out the checks.

There are 3 main ways companies carry out quality checks:

Most good companies will use one or more at lots of different stages of production.

1) Use measuring and calibrating tools.

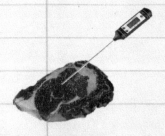

For example a meat probe could be used to check the temperature of cooked meat to ensure that it is at the correct temperature, or a thermometer can be placed on the grill to check that the grill is the correct temperature. Carrying out these checks before using or serving the meat would ensure that no customers get undercooked food.

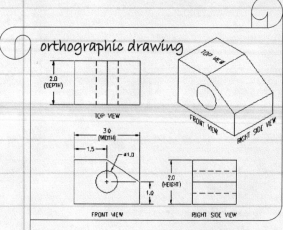

orthographic drawing

2) Use technical drawings to specifying key features

For many manufactured products this will be the first quality control point, using a diagram such as an **orthographic drawing** to specify all the required details.

3) Use agreed quality samples to check the product against.

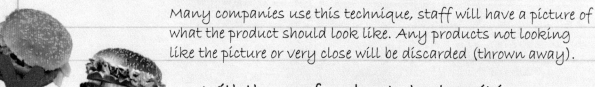

Many companies use this technique, staff will have a picture of what the product should look like. Any products not looking like the picture or very close will be discarded (thrown away).

With the use of modern technology it is now possible for computers to be used to do this job.

Components

Components is a term used to describe the different parts of a product. Some parts are made by the manufacturer themselves and some are bought in separately (called standard or pre-manufactured components).

Some benefits to using standard components are that:
1. It can speed up the manufacturing process as less parts need to be made.
2. Reduces production costs as less tools and staff are needed.
3. Can save storage space because less materials are needed.

Some disadvantages of using standard components are:
1. The manufacturer can not be certain of the quality.
2. Manufacturing may be held up waiting for delivery of components

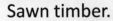

Some of the most common standard components are things such as:

➢ Fasteners (nuts, bolts, screws and washers etc),
➢ Standard parts (zips, ink, welding rods etc),
➢ Basic ingredients (flour, sugar, salt etc),
➢ Thread and fabric,
➢ Buttons,
➢ Standard paper sizes (A5, A4, A3, A2, A1, A0),
➢ Sawn timber.

Smart Materials

Smart materials are materials that can change their properties and/or characteristics as a result of external stimuli. An example of this, are thermo-chromic materials that can change colour when temperature changes. This is used in some kettles to visually show when it is hot or cold.

Is your egg cooked? Thermochromic ink that only appears when your egg is cooked.

Thermochromic Materials and inks

Materials or inks that change colour with temperature

Kettles that can change colour to show how hot or cold they are.

Thermometer that changes colour with temperature..

SMA's are used as triggers to start sprinklers in fire alarm systems, controllers for hot water valves in showers or coffee machines as well as for spectacle frames

Shape-Memory Alloys (SMA)

These are metals that when put in hot water return to their original shape.

Glasses that when you sit on them or stand on them, you can just put them in hot water and they will go back to their original shape.

Nomex®

Nomex is a fabric that when exposed to intense heat like in a fire, it carbonises. This increases the protective barrier between the heat source and the user, helping to reduce burn injury and providing valuable time to work or escape. Nomex is used on fireman's uniforms.

Product Development Stages

Product development is not to be confused with **design development** as they are both very different.

Product development is where a new product is created for resale.

Design development happens during the product development process, this is where designs are created, adapted and improved.

No.	The Stages	What happens
1	Client brief is set	The client/customer tells the designer what they want.
2	Research is carried out	The designer carries out research such as material research, consumer surveys.
3	Specifications are developed	The designer uses the client brief and their research to write a list of things that the product they make will have to fulfil.
4	Designs are developed	Initial ideas are created
5	Designs are presented to the client	The initial ideas are shown to the client from stage one to get their opinions.
6	Designs are modified	Designs are developed/changed based on the clients opinions.
7	Prototype created	A one-off working model of the product is created for testing.
8	Testing	The product is tested to see if it fulfils all of the specifications created in stage 3.
9	Production planning	Once a successful prototype has been made a plan of all the steps needed to make the product and materials needed is created
10	Manufacturing	The product is made, usually in batch production.

Used for:
- Text messaging,
- Video calling,
- Speech calls,
- Emailing,
- Updating social media,
- Sending pictures

To customers, suppliers or co-workers etc

Used for:
- Programming robotic machines or processes

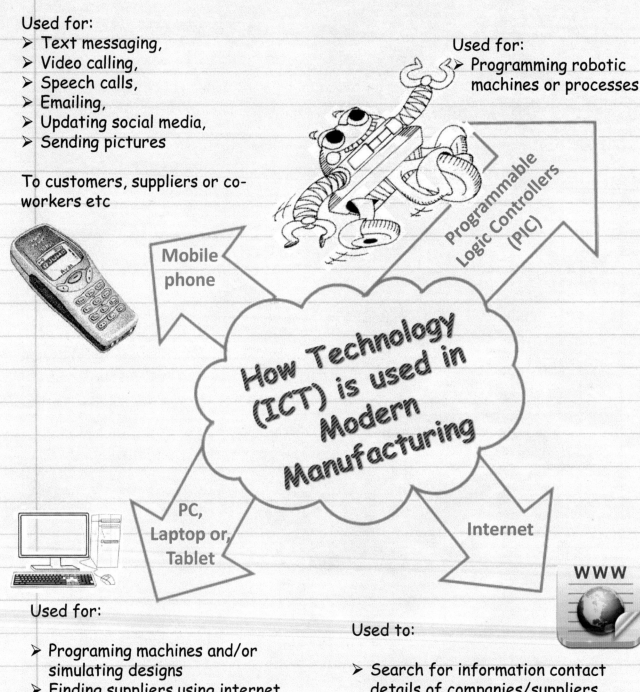

Programmable Logic Controllers (PlC)

Mobile phone

How Technology (ICT) is used in Modern Manufacturing

PC, Laptop or, Tablet

Internet

WWW

Used for:

- Programing machines and/or simulating designs
- Finding suppliers using internet search engines
- Using spreadsheets or other software to manage finances.
- Create digital designs or CAD models.
- Communicating with customers, suppliers etc via internet, social media or video chat.
- Marketing products, on the internet.
- Programming CAM equipment i.e 3D printer, laser cutter etc

Used to:

- Search for information contact details of companies/suppliers,
- Carry out online consumer surveys,
- Communicate to customers & suppliers via e-mail, social media, video chat etc.
- Research materials, manufacturing processes, and/or suppliers.
- Order materials or supplies online.

CAD/CAM

CAD = Computer Aided Design, this is the software used to create a 3D model or file for a CAM device

CAM = Computer Aided Manufacture, this is the machine that uses the CAD file to create a component or product.

CAD/CAM is a very popular and fast growing manufacturing and prototyping technique. Though it is not suitable for all types of manufacture so its is important that the manufacturers consider all the pro's and con's before selecting a CAD/CAM process.

CAD/CAM

Pro's

✓ Designs can be changed easily with CAD software.
✓ Design ideas can be created using CAM almost instantly.
✓ CAD designs can be saved and created whenever necessary using CAM equipment.
✓ Skilled workers are not required to create products/operate CAM.
✓ Workers can be paid less as they are not highly skilled staff.
✓ CAM equipment can run 24/7 with no holidays or breaks.
✓ CAM equipment can produce high amounts of product at a fast rate.
✓ Reduced amount of waste as CAM is very accurate.

Con's

✓ The software and CAM equipment can be very expensive.
✓ Staff will need to be trained to use the CAD/CAM equipment or software, this can also be expensive.
✓ Machines will need servicing.
✓ Manufacturer can not operate if machines or computers break.
✓ If a machine is not set up correctly before use a high number of faulty products can be made in a short amount of time, costing lots of money.

Types of CAM

There are many different CAM tools on the market though some of the most common are:

Laser Cutter: These machines are becoming more affordable and can cut or engrave on a wide range of materials such as wood, plastic, and fabric. They can also engrave on glass and metals. They use a high power laser to do this.

3D Printer: Once called rapid prototyping machines these machines are anything but rapid. Able to make 3D items from a range of materials depending on the type of the machine. Using ribbons or wires of plastics such as ABS which are melted onto a bed in many thin layers. These are very hard wearing and can be used almost like the real product.

CNC Router: These machines have a spinning cutting tool like a drill bit, unlike a laser cutter they can cut more 3D shapes. They can cut a wide range of materials too like, wood, metal, foam etc.

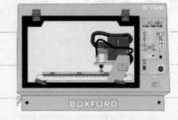

Page:9

Materials: Plastics

Thermoplastics

	PLASTIC	PROPERTIES	USES
USED IN SCHOOL	Polymethyl-methacrylate (Acrylic or PMMA)	Rigid, hard, can be clear, very durable outside, polishes to a high shine.	Illuminated signs, windows, baths,
	Polyvinyl chloride (PVC)	Rigid, quite hard, good chemical resistance, tough.	Pipes, guttering, window, frames,
	Polyethylene (polythene)	Flexible, soft, good chemical resistance, feels waxy	Food bags, buckets, bowls, bottles.
	Polyamide (nylon)	Tough, self lubricating, resists wear, good chemical resistance	Gear wheels, bearings tights, combs
	Polystyrene	Lightweight, hard, rigid, can be clear, good water resistance	Model kits, utensils, containers, packaging
	Expanded Polystyrene	Very lightweight, floats, good heat insulator	Insulation, packaging

	PLASTIC	PROPERTIES	USES
USED IN INDUSTRY	Polyethylene teraphthalate (PET)	Tough, clear, lightweight,	Fizzy drinks bottles
	Polypropylene	Lightweight, flexible, resists cracking and tearing	Climbing ropes, crisp packets
	Acrylonitrile butadiene styrene (ABS)	Very tough, scratch resistant, good chemical resistance	Casings for cameras, kettles, vacuum cleaners

Thermoplastic – Is a plastic that can be heated and reshaped many times.

Thermosetting plastic – Is a plastic that once shaped can not be reshaped. Its good for things that get hot like irons, kettles etc.

Thermosetting plastics

	PLASTIC	PROPERTIES	USES
USED IN SCHOOL	Polyester resin (mixed with glass fibre - GRP)	Hard, rigid, brittle, tough when mixed with glass or carbon fibres	Boat and car bodies, paper weights
	Epoxy resin (Araldite)	Strong, good chemical and heat resistance, sticks to other materials well	Adhesive encapsulating electronic components
USED IN INDUSTRY	Polyethylene teraphthalate (PET)	Rigid, hard scratch resistant, water and stain resistant	Table ware, laminate top coating
	Urea formaldehyde	Rigid, hard, strong, heat resistant, does not bend when heated, good electrical insulator	Electrical plugs and sockets, door knobs

Materials: Metals

Ferrous

Contain Iron

Will rust easily

Type	Picture	Uses
Cast Iron		Very strong. Cannot be bent. Can be cast e.g. Vices
Mild Steel		Tough. Easy to shape e.g. Nuts and bolts
High Carbon Steel		Very hard. Difficult to cut e.g. High speed cutting blade

Non - Ferrous

Does not Contain Iron

Will not rust easily

Type	Picture	Uses
Aluminium		Strong but very light. Polishes well e.g. saucepan
Copper		Good conductor of heat & electricity. Easily joined. E.g. circuit board, piping
Lead		Very heavy. Soft e.g. Car battery
Tin		Very soft, light. Good to coat other materials e.g. Food cans

Alloys

Are a mix of two or more metals

Provide more strength

Type	Picture	Uses
Brass (copper & Zinc)		Decorative Items:- Handles and Knockers
Solder (Tin & Lead) Building Circuit Boards		Used to join components to tracking when heated

Materials: Woods

Hardwood

Comes from trees which lose their leaves in autumn (deciduous)

Typically the wood from these trees are tougher and the fibres are more dense than softwoods.

Type	Picture	Uses
Mahogany		Indoor furniture
Beech		Workbenches. Tools.
Oak		Outdoor furniture

Softwood

Comes from trees which keep their leaves in autumn (coniferous).

These trees are fast growing trees that produce woods that is much softer than hardwoods.

Type	Picture	Uses
Pine		Cheap furniture. Construction work.
Red Cedar		Wall panels. Sheds/fences.

Manufactured boards

These are man made woods. Each one is made slightly differently.

Plywood

Blockboard

Chipboard

Medium Density Fibreboard (MDF)

- Come in large sheets of uniform thickness
- Not affected by humidity
- Can be used with veneers
- Do not have grain structure
- More easily worked than natural timbers

Materials: Fabrics

Page:13

The greater the number of blobs the greater the property in question, e.g.
For weight: ● indicates light weight, ●●●● indicates heavy weight
For inflammability: ● indicates not very inflammable, ●●●● indicates very inflammable

Name and composition	Weight	Drape	Appearance	Strength	Absorbency	Inflammability	Aftercare	Cost
Calico unbleached 100 % cotton	●●●●	●●	stiffish weave, creamy colour	●●●●	●●●●	●●●●	cotton wash, hot iron, may shrink	●
Calico bleached 100% cotton	●●●●	●●	stiffish weave, white	●●●●	●●●●	●●●●	cotton wash, hot iron	●
Cotton heavy or medium duty 100% cotton	●●●●	●●●	softer weave than calico, creamy or white: plain colours or coloured prints	●●●●	●●●●	●●●●	cotton wash, hot iron, if pre-shrunk won't shrink again	●●●
Cotton lawn 100% cotton	●●	●●●●	soft but slightly stiff weave, white/colours, slightly see-through	●●●	●●●●	●●●●	cotton wash, hot iron, damp iron	●●/●●●
Muslin 100% cotton	●	●●●	very soft loose weave, creamy or white, more see-through than lawn	●	●●●●	●●●●	cotton wash, hot iron, take care, reshape, damp iron	●
Polyester (plain weave) 100% polyester	●●	●●●	varied	●●●●	●	●●●● melts	synthetics wash, polyester iron, use fabric softener	●●●
Polyester-cotton (plain weave) 65% polyester / 35% cotton	●●	●●●	smoothish plain weave, plain or patterned colours	●●●●	●●	●●●● some melt	synthetics wash, polyester iron, minimum iron	●●●
Nylon, waterproof 100% nylon	●	●●	coated woven fabric, plain colours	●●●●	N/A	●●●● melts	low synthetics wash, cool or no iron	●●●
Nylon, net 100% nylon	●	●	net fabric, quite stiff and brittle, variety of colours, Lurex and rainbow net also available	●	N/A	●●●● melts	low synthetics wash, no iron	●●/●●●
Fur fabric 67% acrylic 33% modified acrylic	●●●	●●	woven or knitted, variety of colours and patterns	●●	●	acrylic ●●●● modified acrylic ●	synthetics wash, no iron, brush up pile	●●●●
Metallic fabric 55% metallic polyester 45% nylon	●	●●●	usually woven, often silver or gold	●●	●	●●●● melts	synthetics wash, no iron	●●●●
Hessian 100 % jute	●●/●●●	●●/●●●	woven, variety of weights, colours and textures, paper-backed available, rather scratchy	●●●	●●●●	●●●●	low cotton wash, medium iron, reshape	●●●
Silk (pongee) 100% silk	●	●●●●	woven, smooth weave, variety of light/fine weights	●●●	●●●●	●●	often hand wash, cool iron	●●●/●●●●
Wool (flannel) 100 % wool	●●/●●●	●●●	woven, slightly textured, variety of colours	●●●	●●●	●●	wool wash or no wash, warm iron	●●●/●●●●
Vilene	varies	N/A	non-woven interfacing, different weights, usually black or white, iron on or stitch in	●/●●●	N/A	●	as items fused to but can become unfused in hot washes	●

Plastic forming

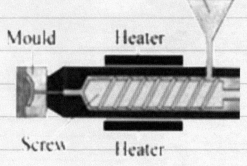

Hopper

Mould   Heater

Screw   Heater

Injection Moulding

Plastic pellets are placed in the hopper. As the screw turns the heaters melt these pellets into a liquid. This liquid is then pushed by the screw into the mould, where it would cool and become solid and shaped.

This process is often selected as it can be used to create very intricate designs with unusually shapes, and very little plastic is wasted. There is a little mark tail left where the plastic is injected called a spru, this has to be cut off and often leaves a small mark.

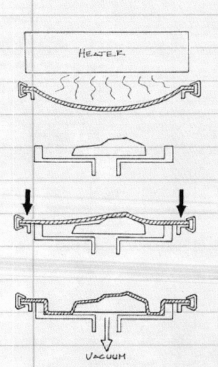

Vacuum forming

A mould of the required shape has to be made and placed inside a vacuum chamber. Plastic sheets are clamped over the vacuum above the mould.

The plastic is then heated air is sucked out of the vacuum which caused the plastic to form around the mould.

This process is often selected for making packaging as it is very cheap compared to injection moulding, however it is limited to producing hollow products from thin plastics and produces quiet a large amount of waste.

Lin bending

A sheet of plastic can be bent using a strip heater.,

The strip heater has one straight line of heating element that gets hot and heats a straight line on the plastic. This plastic can then be bent along this line.

acrylic

element

adjustable rests

This process is often selected for making leaflet stands or point of sale units in shops. It is the cheapest method of shaping plastics.

Plastic Forming Summary

Plastic forming processes				
Process	Advantages	Disadvantages	Plastics used	Applications
Injection moulding	Ideal for mass or continual production – low unit cost for high volumes. Precision moulding – high quality surface finish or texture can be added.	High initial set-up costs as moulds expensive to develop and produce	Nylon, ABS, PS, HDPE, PP.	Casings for electronic products, containers for storage and packaging
Blow moulding	Intricate shapes can be formed. Can produce hollow shapes with thin walls to reduce weight and material costs. Ideal for mass or continual production.	High initial set-up costs as moulds expensive to develop and produce. Large amounts of waste material produced.	HDPE, LDPE, PET, PP, PS, PVC	Plastic bottles and containers of all sizes and shapes, e.g., fizzy drinks and shampoo bottles.
Vacuum forming	Ideal for batch production – inexpensive. Easy to make moulds. Moulds can be easily modified.	Mould needs to be accurate to prevent 'webbing' from occurring.	Acrylic, HIP (high impact polysty-rene), PVC	Chocolate box trays, yoghurt pots, blister packs.
Line bending	Ideal for one off or small batches of products. Low cost for machines and tools.	Only able to produce folds in plastics	Acrylic, HIP (high impact polysty-rene), PVC	Point of sale displays, storage products, etc.

Glass forming

Float glass process

Float glass process – float glass is a process which 90% of today's flat glass is manufactured. The raw materials are properly weighted and mixed and then introduced into a furnace where they are melted at 1500° C. The molten glass then flows from the glass furnace onto a bath of molten tin in a continuous ribbon. When leaving the bath of molten tin the glass has cooled down sufficiently to pass to an annealing chamber called a lehr. Here it is cooled under controlled temperatures, until it is essentially at room temperature.

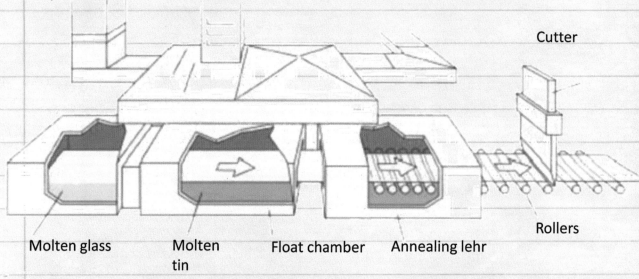

Molten glass   Molten tin   Float chamber   Annealing lehr   Cutter   Rollers

Blow moulding - glass

The entire process of bottle making is almost fully automated. An automated feeder separates a stream of molten glass into individual gobs. These are then dropped through tubes in a moving track. The gob is shaped into what looks like a short bottle with thick walls and is called a parison. The parison is transferred to a final mould made of iron, which moves up and clamps around the glass. Air is blown into the glass till it acquires the final shape of the mould. This procedure involving expansion is called blowing. The bottle is then released from the mould and annealed.

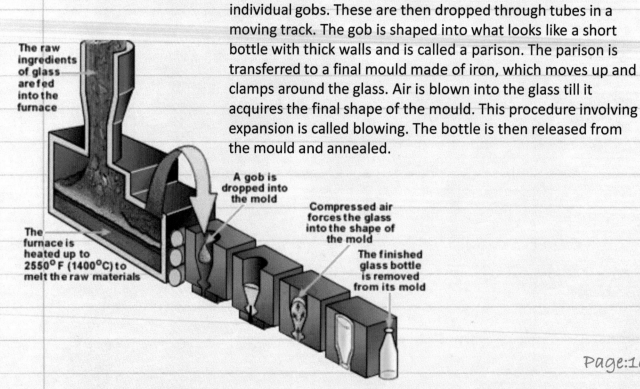

The raw ingredients of glass are fed into the furnace

The furnace is heated up to 2550°F (1400°C) to melt the raw materials

A gob is dropped into the mold

Compressed air forces the glass into the shape of the mold

The finished glass bottle is removed from its mold

Metal forming

Metal Casting

Metal is heated until it melts and it then poured into a mould and left to cool. It can then be annealed or put through other processes to work with it.

Male mould

Press moulding

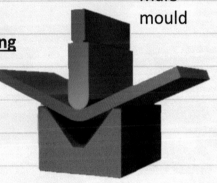

Sheets of metal can be press moulded. Two moulds are needed a male and female, the metal is the squashed in-between both.

Female mould

Die Cutting

A mould of the shape required is made from tool steel and a machine or mechanical press is used to stamp these out on sheets of metal cutting out the required shape.

Soldering

Soldering is widely used to join electrical components to circuit boards though can be used for joining metals together too, such as in plumbing.

It works by melting a bit of solder (a metal with a low melting point) and using it as a sort of glue to join two other metals together. It is not a very strong joint but its suitable for things that don't have a lot of movement.

soldering iron

solder wire

Metal joining

flux is a substance used which facilitates soldering, brazing, and welding by chemically cleaning the metals to be joined

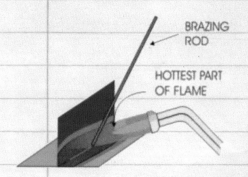

BRAZING ROD

HOTTEST PART OF FLAME

Brazing is the joining of metals through the use of heat and a filler metal or alloy (acting like glue), which has a lower melting point than the base metals being joined. This is performed at reasonably low temperatures (between 450 – 1000ºC) reducing the possibility of warping, overheating or melting the metals being joined. Brazing is ideally suited to the **joining of dissimilar metals**. You can easily join assemblies that combine ferrous with nonferrous metals, and metals with widely varying melting points.

Brazed joints are **strong,** i.e. on non-ferrous metals and steels, the tensile strength of a properly made joint will often last longer than **that of the metals joined.**

Soldering is a process where heat is applied to the parts to be joined, causing the solder to melt and be drawn into the joint by capillary action and to bond to the materials to be joined. After the metal cools, the resulting joints are not as strong as the base metal, but have adequate strength, electrical conductivity, and water-tightness for many uses such as joining copper, brass, tinplate or light steelwork, and is the normal way of joining electronic circuit components.

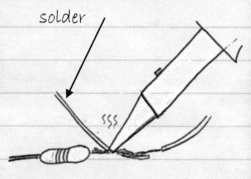

solder

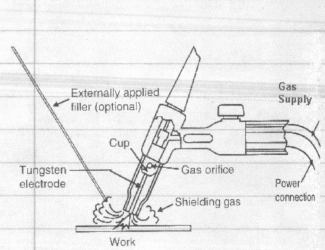

Externally applied filler (optional)

Cup

Tungsten electrode

Gas orifice

Shielding gas

Work

Gas Supply

Power connection

Welding - Process of permanently joining two or more metal parts, by melting both materials. The molten materials quickly cool, and the two metals are permanently bonded. Spot welding and seam welding are two very popular methods used for sheet metal parts.

Oxy-acetylene welding uses a very hot flame.

Electric arc welding a spark is used to heat the metal. In both processes a filler rod may used as well to get a really strong joint.

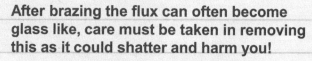

WARNING

After brazing the flux can often become glass like, care must be taken in removing this as it could shatter and harm you!

Be careful of unattended metal work as it may still be very hot!

Textile Processes

Batik

Batik is a traditional Chinese folk art which combines painting and dyeing. This is traditionally made by dipping a specially designed knife into melted wax and painting various patterns on pieces of white cloth. The wax stays on the cloth and often cracks after it hardens. The cloth is then dyed; the dyes seep into the cracks and make fine lines. When the wax is removed, beautiful patterns appear on the cloth. Batik cloth can be made into garments, scarves, bags, table-cloths, bedspreads, curtains, and other decorative items.

Below is an examples of this technique in use:

CAD/CAM Embroidery sewing machine

Embroidery is the art of decorating fabric or other materials with designs stitched in strands of thread or yarn using a needle. Embroidery may also incorporate other materials such as metal strips, pearls, beads, quills, and sequins.

In recent years it has been possible to use CAD to embroider by using a specialised machine (CAM) that can read the CAD file (computerised design) to automatically create a stitched design.

Below is an example of embroidery used in today's fashion industry to create a trendy colorful pattern.

Below is an examples of this technique in use:

Embellisher

This is a fascinating machine. It doesn't use thread at all, just 7 barbed needles to "felt" fibres, threads, and fabrics all together to create fabric art. These pieces can be created and used as is, or quilted, then used as wall art, or as part of wearable art, tote bags, purses, or just appliqués.

Below is an example of using the embellisher to join different coloured felt together, from this example you will be able to note the way the machine pulls the fabric from underneath through the top layer of fabric. It is also this effect that some artists like to make various patterns in their work as can also be seen in the picture at the bottom of the page.

Heat press

Heat pressing is simple and has become the standard for quick, high definition, high quality, low cost imprinting of a vast range of materials.

A **heat press** is a machine used that presses a transfer onto a printable substrate. Using high temperatures and heavy pressures for a certain amount of time, the transfer is permanently embedded into the product.

Textile Interfacings

quality	description	fabric types	method and care
H200 Iron-on Interfacing	Light control suitable for small parts such as collars, cuffs, pockets and facings on dresses and blouses. Easy to iron on and comfortable to wear. **Colours: white and black.** 90cm-wide, sold by the metre.	Use on lightweight fabrics such as cotton, polyester, silk and jersey.	Use **Dry Heat Method**, iron setting - wool. Glide iron over slowly 5 or 6 times. ⬜40 Ⓟ 🔥 8 secs
G405 Softline Iron-on Interfacing	Soft versatile interfacing used on whole jacket fronts and small parts such as collars and pocket flaps. Good shape-retaining qualities. **Colours: White and charcoal.** 90cm-wide, sold by the metre.	Light to medium-weight fabrics such as wool, poplin, flannel, gabardine, satin and silk.	Use **Damp Cloth Method**, iron setting - wool/cotton. Press each area for 10-12 secs. ⬜40 Ⓟ 🔥 12 secs + damp cloth
H410 Softline Iron-on Interfacing	A soft interfacing with stabilising vertical threads, designed to give a traditional tailored effect. Suitable for whole jackets fronts, plus smaller parts such as collars, lapels, pocket flaps and slits. Retains perfect shape, comfortable to wear. **Colours: White and black.** 90cm-wide, sold by the metre.	Suitable for many fabrics from light to heavy-weight, such as wool, gabardine, tweed, worsted, silk, satin or double jersey.	**Important:** When cutting out, the threads along the grain must follow the grain of the fabric. Use **Damp Cloth Method**, iron setting - wool/cotton. Press each area for 10-12 secs. ⬜40 Ⓟ 🔥 12 secs + damp cloth
H250 Standard Iron-on Interfacing	A crisp, stable interfacing for shaped cuffs, belts, bodices, hats and textile crafts. Easy to apply, gives long-lasting shape. **Colours: White and charcoal.** 90cm-wide, sold by the metre.	Use on light to medium-weight fabrics such as cotton, linen, denim, poplin and baby cord.	Use **Dry Heat Method**, iron setting - wool. Glide iron very slowly over each area 5-6 times, so each area receives 8 secs of heat. ⬜60 Ⓟ 🔥 8 secs
H608 Stretch Iron-on Interfacing	Lightweight and extremely elastic, with very soft handle, provides perfect support whilst retaining comfort. Can be used on whole jacket fronts, plus small parts such as collars, cuffs, pocket and flaps. **Colours: White and charcoal.** 90cm-wide, sold by the metre.	Light to heavy-weight elastic and jersey fabrics, such as single knit, double knit, velour and sweater, plus stable outer fabrics too.	**Important:** Cut out all pieces following grain of fabric to retain elastic qualities. Use **Damp Cloth Method**, iron setting - wool/cotton. Press each area for 12 secs. ⬜40 Ⓟ 🔥-🔥 12 secs + damp cloth
Fuse-and-Fold Iron-on Band Interfacing	A triple-slotted tape ideal for waistbands. Easy to use; comes in three widths. Simply iron on fabric and cut out. Slots give an accurate guide for folding and stitching. Sold by the metre in **white and charcoal**. Finished widths: 25mm, 30mm and 35mm wide.	Gives a firm finish for most fabrics.	Use **Dry Heat Method**, iron setting - wool. Glide iron slowly over each area 5-6 times, pressing firmly, so each area receives 8 secs of heat. ⬜95 Ⓟ 🔥 8 secs
Wundaweb® For Iron-on Hems and Seams	A fast and easy transparent tape for invisibly fixing hems without sewing. Ideal for clothing, soft furnishings, crafts and applying trims. "Extra Strong" Wundaweb® is available for heavy-weight fabrics. Sold in pre-packs: 20mm-wide by 5m, 10m or 20m. "Extra Strong": 20mm-wide by 3m only.	Perfect for most fabrics. Use standard for light to medium-weight fabrics and "Extra Strong" for medium to heavy-weight fabrics	Press up a 40mm-wide hem. Insert Wundaweb® into hem fold so 4-5mm of fabric remains above and below; press in place using **Damp Cloth Method**, iron setting - wool/cotton. Press down on each area for 10 secs. ⬜60 Ⓟ 🔥-🔥 10 secs + damp cloth
Bondaweb® For Creative Appliqué and other Crafts	A transparent double-sided adhesive on a paper backing for fast and easy appliqué on clothing, soft furnishings and other crafts. No shifting when stitching around edges. Sold by the metre, 90cm-wide and 45cm-wide. Pre-packed: 1m by 18cm-wide.	Suitable for most fabrics, and also raffia, cardboard, paper, wood and, at lower temperatures, leather.	Draw motif on to paper side of Bondaweb®; cut out roughly. Using **Dry Heat Method**, iron setting - wool, press down for 5 secs. Cut out motif; peel off backing. Place motif adhesive side down on garment; using **Damp Cloth Method**, iron setting: wool/cotton, press down for 10 secs. ⬜60 Ⓟ 🔥 5 secs 🔥-🔥 10 secs + damp cloth

TIP: "Iron-on" interfacings are the easiest to use and are the ones recommended for the novice stitcher.

TIP: Use a firm, even surface for fusing, such as a table. If you use an ironing board, you can improve the result by placing a pressing cloth below.

Graphics Processes

Letterpress

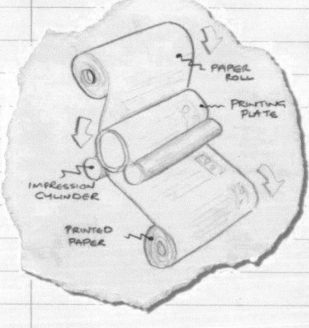

- Letterpress is a form of **relief printing**. The printing area stands above the non-printing area.
- The printing area is inked and then **pressed** against the paper
- This process is quite slow.
- **Rotary letterpress** is used to **speed** things up. It uses an aluminium plate which holds and text wrapped around a **drum** and is rolled over the paper
- Letterpress was widely used up **until the late 1980's**
- Rotary letterpress is a **very economical** way of producing text which is frequently reprinted
- **CAD and DTP** are **not compatible** with Letterpress, so newspapers are now printed using Lithography
- Letterpress is not suitable for colour pictures, photos or fine detail.
- Letterpress is use for printing some books and some packaging

Screen printing

- Screen printing uses a **stencil** through which ink is forced.
- The holes in the stencil are the **same shape** as the image to be printed
- The stencil can be made of **different materials**, eg paper, thin card and special photographic materials.
- The stencil is held in place by a fine **nylon mesh.**
- Screen printing is limited to **simple shapes.**
- Screen printing can be used to print on rough or uneven surfaces...Eg. **T-Shirts**, **glass bottles** and **PVC signs**

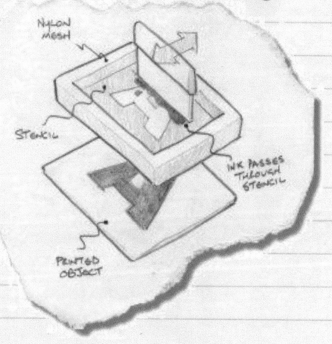

Graphics Processes

Gravure

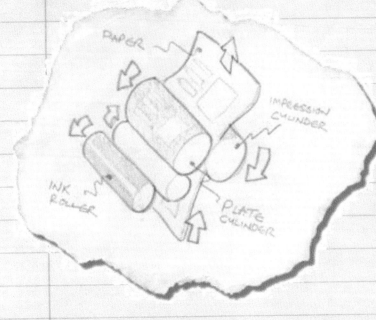

- Gravure is a high speed rotary process
- Unlike letterpress the print surface is lower than the non-printing surface
- Ink fills the gaps in the printing plates. Paper is pressed against the plate by an impression cylinder.
- Unlike lithography the printing plate is made of copper which is more durable than aluminium. However, gravure printing plates are more expensive to make.
- Gravure is expensive to set up and is only used for print runs of over about half a million copies
- Gravure is used for very high quality printing.

Offset Lithography

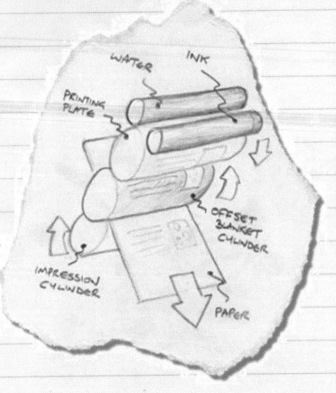

Printing using lithographic printing

1. Lithographic relies on a the ink an water not mixing.

2. The image is put onto an aluminium printing plate using ultra violet light shinning through a negative.

3. The plate is coated in a chemical that makes the image area attractive to oil and therefore the ink.

4. Water is used to repel the ink where it is not wanted.

5. Each colour is added to the image using s different set of negatives and plates.

Graphics Processes Summary

Process	Lithography	Letterpress	Gravure	Screen Printing
Applications	Magazines, posters, CD leaflets, brochures, newspapers, business cards, stationary.	Books with large amounts of text, business cards, letterheads	Expensive magazines, stamps, high quality art and photographic books, packaging	T-shirts, posters, plastic and metal signage, point-of-sale-displays
Advantages	Good reproduction quality especially photographs, cheap printing process, widely used, high printing speeds, print on a wide range of papers.	Dense ink gives good quality prints. Less paper wastage than other processes.	Consistent colour, high printing speeds, very high quality, ink dries on evaporation, good results on cheaper paper.	Economical for short runs, stencils easy to produce, can print on virtually any material
Disadvantages	Plate life of only 150,000 but is easily replaced, paper can stretch due to dampening, colour variation due to water/ink mixture	Slow process, not good for colour pics, high cost.	Printing plates and cylinders very expensive, only good for long print runs	Low output, difficult to achieve fine detail, print requires a long drying time

Electronic Concepts

Volts – (the symbol – V)

Units of electrical pressure, meaning the difference in potential between the positive and negative terminals of the power source.

Amp (the symbol - A)

This is the unit of current, meaning the rate that electricity flows around a circuit

Ohm – (the symbol Ω)

This is the unit of resistance within a circuit.

Materials that have a high resistance are called insulators, those with low are called conductors, and if a material has no resistance it is called a superconductor.

Watt (the symbol – W)

This is the unit of power this is worked out by Voltage (V) X Current (A)

Farad (the symbol – F)

This is the unit of capacitance, which is the amount of electrical charge that can be stored in a capacitor

Coulomb (the symbol - C)
1 coulomb is the amount of electric charge carried by a current of 1 ampere flowing for 1 second.

It can also be defined in terms of capacitance and voltage, where one coulomb is defined as one farad of capacitance times one volt of electric potential difference:

Key concept

Ohms law defines the relationship between Voltage (V), Current (I) and Resistance (R) as:

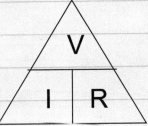

Time constant can be calculated with:

T (seconds) = C (farads) X R (ohms)

The following symbols and prefixes are used throughout electronics:

Symbol	Prefix	Multiplier	
G	giga	one thousand million	10^9
M	mega	one million	10^6
k	kilo	one thousand	10^3
m	milli	one thousandth	10^{-3}
µ	micro	one millionth	10^{-6}
n	nano	one thousand millionth	10^{-9}

Electronic Components

Resistor colour code

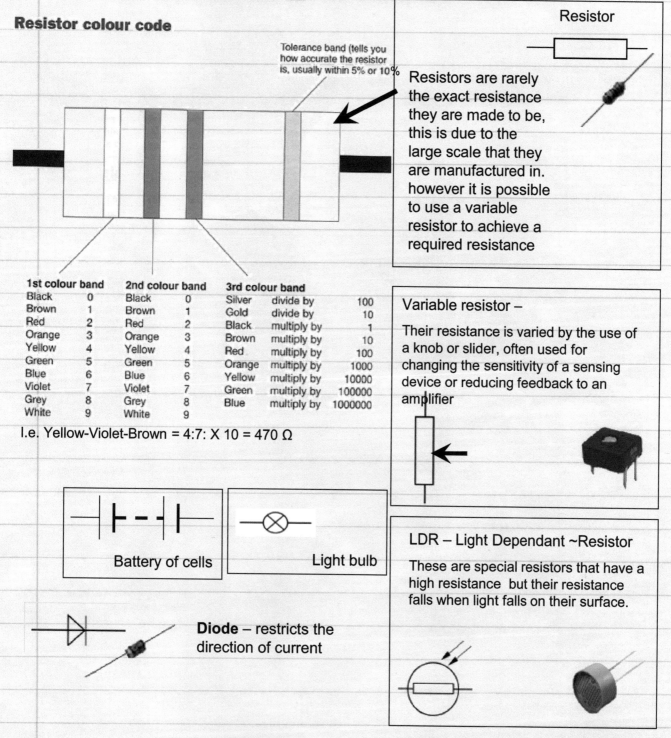

Tolerance band (tells you how accurate the resistor is, usually within 5% or 10%

Resistor

Resistors are rarely the exact resistance they are made to be, this is due to the large scale that they are manufactured in. however it is possible to use a variable resistor to achieve a required resistance

1st colour band		2nd colour band		3rd colour band		
Black	0	Black	0	Silver	divide by	100
Brown	1	Brown	1	Gold	divide by	10
Red	2	Red	2	Black	multiply by	1
Orange	3	Orange	3	Brown	multiply by	10
Yellow	4	Yellow	4	Red	multiply by	100
Green	5	Green	5	Orange	multiply by	1000
Blue	6	Blue	6	Yellow	multiply by	10000
Violet	7	Violet	7	Green	multiply by	100000
Grey	8	Grey	8	Blue	multiply by	1000000
White	9	White	9			

I.e. Yellow-Violet-Brown = 4:7: X 10 = 470 Ω

Variable resistor –

Their resistance is varied by the use of a knob or slider, often used for changing the sensitivity of a sensing device or reducing feedback to an amplifier

Battery of cells

Light bulb

LDR – Light Dependant ~Resistor

These are special resistors that have a high resistance but their resistance falls when light falls on their surface.

Diode – restricts the direction of current

LED – Light Emitting Diode

Anode   Cathode

Flat

–

+

A Cell

The standard voltage of a dry battery is 1.5V. By connecting them together in series you can achieve a higher voltage.

Coursework: 1A

Unit B231 *1A Study of a Manufactured Product*

For this piece of coursework you will investigate how a product has developed over the years.

To start with you must select one of the products listed below by OCR and two modern equivalent products that you will use to compare it against. There are more products that you can choose from, but the 9 below are the easiest to gain full marks with.

1920s Kettle	1940s Television	1950s Radio
1940s Sewing machine	1940s Bakelite telephone	1990s PC's
1940s Bicycle	1950s Camera	1970s Walkman

You will be marked on the following 4 areas:

Mark criteria

Impact of modern technologies

Gives a fully detailed description of:

- The impact of modern technologies, smart materials and components on their development
- The advantages and disadvantages that the use of modern technology has brought to society.

[7 8 9]

Materials and Components

Gives a fully detailed and justified explanation of the use of materials and components and their:

- Properties
- Characteristics
- Performance; and
- Cost;

Specialist terms will be used appropriately and correctly. The information will be presented in a structured format. The candidate can demonstrate the accurate use of spelling, punctuation and grammar.

[7 8 9]

Manufacturing processes

Gives a fully detailed and justified explanation of the:

- Manufacturing processes used.

[5 6]

Modify design solutions

Suggests and explains in detail:

- Modifications to design solutions
- Sustainability issues.

[5 6]

Impact of Modern Technologies

On your front cover place a picture of the three developments of your chosen product showing the years they were manufactured.

1

For the first section of your 1A coursework you should write a paragraph giving general information about how the product you are investigating has changed and what new things were invented that made this possible. This can be things like 'new manufacturing tools have been created that have made it possible for the product to become smaller and more compact.' though make sure to give more than one example.

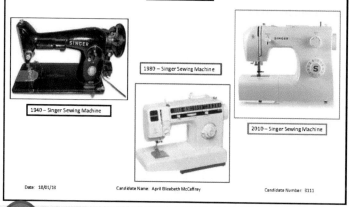

Development of the 1940's Sewing Machine

1940 – Singer Sewing Machine

1980 – Singer Sewing Machine

2010 – Singer Sewing Machine

Date: 18/01/13   Candidate Name: April Elizabeth McCaffrey   Candidate Number: 3111

2

You must also provide some research into smart materials explain what they are and how they have been used in the development of your product.

3

Finally for this section, you must explain the benefits and disadvantages of using all this modern technology to make products on society. This means the effects it has on our environment and peoples lives.

Remember you must explain your reasons, Just because you think something is an advantage doesn't mean other people will think it is. For example with modern technology more machines are used to do jobs. A manufacture will think this is good because they don't need to pay people. Workers will think this is bad because they have less jobs.

Effects of Modern Technology on the Development of Products

Modern technology has increased into a new era, breaking many different ideas in order to improvise and improve the lives of everyday people. When looking at the modern sewing machine compared to the sewing machine of the 1940s, it is easy to see how design, components and material has changed.

In the 1940s, most of the sewing machines were usually made out of iron; a sturdy metal that could last up to a few years. However, iron does not work well against water or oxygen, causing it to rust under the influence and over time. Taking in the disadvantag...

lightweight,
that are ligh...
injection-mo...
plate specifi...

These impro...
what could I...
materials an...
example, Ke...
basis and so...
are other sm...
been modifi...

The smart m...
the 1940s m...
for the circu...
properties. I...
movement c...
the circuit b...

Date: 18/01/13

Effects of Modern Technology on the Development of Products

Advantages:

As technology increases in our everyday lives, there have been many advantages to the use of machines in factories. For example, using machines as the production of certain products will mean a faster work rate, allowing more of the same product being made in less time than those made by the normal human speed. This means that there is more mass production in less time and more of the product can be sold. Furthermore, having the machines create the product also means there is no need to pay for labour cost or compensation if there is an accident, so there will be a higher rate for profit as less money will be spent. Lastly, people can be hired to be product designers, and, unlike fifty years ago, they can produce thousands of computer designs that can be processed through and changed quickly and easily. Years before, each design had to be hand drawn over and over again until the project manager found the right one.

Because of the latest inventions and science, items that can be placed in the factories in order to reduce the amount of pollution. This means that more factories can be built without the danger of too much pollution from one company's factories. Science has been a major part of new ways for technology, and have found new materials that can be sustainable, letting different companies to produce their own type of material that can be used over and over again, without the risk of running out.

Disadvantages:

Although there are many advantages to new technology, there are also an equal amount of disadvantages. Using the advantage of less labour costs because machines are taking the work, it also means that there will be many people that will be left jobless because they're no more jobs available for a lot of unqualified workers. Only those who are qualified in mechanics, product design, or other management could be hired in order to repair any machines that break down as well as any part of the product that need a human co-ordinator in order to produce what is needed. Although there will be many jobs available, there are much less available compared to the jobs in a factory of 100 years ago. There could be hundreds of people working on one part of a product; now there is only a group of ten – twenty (at most) to make sure everything runs smoothly for the machines. Then, like on many occasions, the machine was not to run smoothly, thus breaking down, depending on what job it was 'in charge' for, the factory may have to temporally close in order to fix/replace the machine. Replacing the machine can also be shown to be difficult and expensive.

Not only will the factory have problems, but the surrounding area also. Many factories are built on urban landscapes, destroying natural wildlife and polluting other areas. Although science has made breakthroughs on reducing pollution, the amount of factories built makes up for the loss amount. More factories also means more materials. More materials used means that, in a few decades, we can run out of certain natural materials, replacing them with synthetic material which can not be recycled – filling landmines.

Date: 18/01/13   Candidate Name: April Elizabeth McCaffrey   Candidate Number: 3111

Materials & Components

1 For this section of your 1A coursework you need to label the pictures of the 3 products that you are investigating naming the materials and components for all of them.

> Tip. It doesn't matter if you get guess the wrong material as long as you can explain why you think they might have used it well enough.

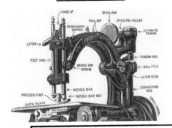

Materials and Components
1940s Sewing Machine

The outer casting, or body, of the 1940s sewing machine was usually made up of iron. Iron would have been very heavy with little resistance to both water and oxygen, meaning it would end up rusting after only a couple of years. It would have also been a burden to move because of it's weight.

Because iron was relatively new in 1940 products, the cost of iron would have been around 20 sterling. Now, it would cost roughly £40 for one sewing machine. 20 sterling was a very expensive price as most workers (with good pay) would have earned roughly 5 sterling a week.

The main shaft, here being the spool-pin, spool-pin holder and the tension rod, were also made up of metal, mainly steel. The steel would be heavy but durable, and would also rust after a few years of use, meaning it would need to be replaced often.

The needle bar and needle bar nut would be made of iron; a tough material that would be good to pierce fabric, but would easily rust and break. It would only take up to a few months before the needle would need to be replaced.

The gears of the 1940s sewing machine, or the looper and rocker, was made out of steel. Again, the steel was very durable and could work well, but it would not last very long as it would rust.

The price of steel would have also

Date: 18/01/13

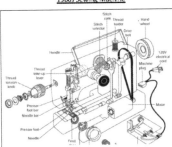

Materials and Components
1980s Sewing Machine

The outer casting of the 1980s sewing machine was usually made out of PVC as it was tough and a good chemical resistance. However, PCV was quite weighty and rigid, meaning that a sudden collision could break the outer casting and expose the inner parts of the sewing machine.

The PVC would have cost roughly £10 - £15 for one sewing machine; this was a moderately high price at the time.

The main shaft was the stitch selector, stitch cam and thread holder, with an early type of nylon that was used for all of these parts. A standard cotton thread was held in this part of the sewing machine.

As nylon was newly invented, it would have been a higher price than all the other materials.

The needle bar would have been made of steel, which would have been strong and heat resistant against the rapid movement, but it would stain and pass any sort of rust over onto the fabric, meaning it would need to be replaced very often.

Steel was only about £5 for a small sheet, to £30 for the largest available, a seemingly acceptable price for the time it was manufactured.

The gears, such as the drive belt, was each made up of different materials. The drive belt was usually made from rubber, which would be useful because of it's flexibility, but would wear down after a while and snap, making it another part that would need

Date: 18/01/13

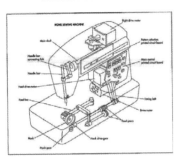

Materials and Components
Modern Sewing Machine

The outer casting of the modern sewing machine are usually made of a strong plastic, such as ABS, which is lightweight, sturdy and crack/chip resistant. This lowers the risk of cracking if it was suddenly dropped/hit. Also, as it is lightweight, it helps the owner move around with the machine without any harm to the person.

ABS has a standard price of £5 - £10, depending on the size of the sheet that is being bought.

The main shaft inside the sewing machine is made of aluminium, but can also be made out of nylon. Both aluminium and nylon are strong materials which are also good wear resistant too. This means that the parts inside the machine will not have to be replaced on a regular basis.

Aluminium has a very high range depending on the size of the sheet, but even a small sheet can be quite expensive being roughly £20. However, a large sheet can cost over £100.

The plastics that are widely available now allows us to use a different range that can be used for each different component. Now, the sewing machine is light-weight, much more durable as a whole and more appealing. However, the price of the sewing machines has increased indefinitely compared to the price of the 1940s and 1980s prices.

Candidate Name: April Elizabeth McCaffrey

The needle bar and connecting link, as well as the needle and feed bar, are all made up of stainless steel, which would stay strong against it's use and resist to the heat when it is in use. It has exactly the same qualities and advantages as the 1980's steel needle, but removes the disadvantage of the steel rusting or scratching, meaning it also does not need to be replaced often.

Stainless steel has also a high price on the market, ranging from £30 - £50.

All the gears of the sewing machine, as well as the bolts and circuit board, are all made out of nylon. Nylon is self-lubricant, meaning that the gears should not rust, and should run smoothly with it's use. They are also tough with good resistance to wearing down.

The price of nylon in modern times has decreased from the 1980s, marketing at £15 - £40.

Candidate Number: 3111

Date: 18/01/13

2 You will then need to explain why the manufacturer has chosen to use this material or component commenting on:

❑ The cost of the material, this does not need to be a price but you should state if the material is expensive or cheap

❑ The properties of the material &
❑ The performance of the material

> Some people do this as one page, and still get full marks

Manufacturing Processes

1 For this section you must identify one or two parts from each of the developments of your product. And name the process used to make them

2 You then need to explain in as much detail as possible how the manufacturing process works, like on page 16 of this book.

3 Once you have done that you will need to explain why the manufacturers chose to make the part in they way you think they did. For this bit it helps to compare the process to an alternative method.

For example comparing wave soldering to hand soldering. In this case its easy to see why the manufacturer of say a Walkman would not use hand soldering, because humans are slow, inefficient and expensive. Wave soldering can be one by a machine very quickly etc.

Manufacturing Process

1940 Sewing Machine

In 1940, the sewing machine was fitted with the first motor. However, even though the industrial revolution had begun, most products were still hand made. The 1940 sewing machine frame was most likely made by sand casting. Sand casting is a cheap and sufficiently refractory even for steel foundry use, meaning it would have been the most suitable in order to preserve the amount of metal used as well as the amount of money it would cost to do so.

There are six steps in this process:

1. Place a pattern in sand to create a mould.
2. Incorporate the pattern and sand in a gating system.
3. Remove the pattern.
4. Fill the mould cavity with molten metal.
5. Allow the metal to cool.
6. Break away the sand mould and remove the casting

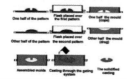

The base of the machine would have most probably been die-cut, a tool that is specifically shaped for a certain job; like shaping the base into what ever design the user wants. After the base is complete, other components like the motor and foot pedal would have been tested, then welded onto the frame before the frame is also welded onto the base.

Welding consists of a small heated electrode which is heated enough to melt the metal that needs to be welded. As the metal melts, it 'sucks' together so when it cools again, it would be fixed together into one piece. Unfortunately, this would make the metal weaker, which is why this was not the method used to make the parts of the machine.

Hand-made process was one of the most dangerous and expensive processes, but was the only one available. It also showed to be good results however as batch production was created though this way. Some machines were available for electrical work, most probably what was used to create the motor, but was still extremely expensive and very hard to maintain as it was a working progress in order to let it become how it is today. Even though paying workers was a lot of profit handed out, paying to keep a machine up and running would have cost a lot more.

Date: 18/01/13   Candidate Name: April Elizabeth McCaffrey   Candidate Number: 3111

Process

...not much that has changed but perhaps what material is used on ...suit board. In modern day sewing machine, they use robotics in ...d wires for protection. However, the 1980s did not have many ...nd tested by people. If there was any fault or problem with the ...rate much power so would not put much risk into the user. ...0s would show live wires. As mentioned before, if the sewing machine was dropped, it would probably crack and/or break, so a live circuit board that has no safety cover would prove to be dangerous to some extent.

A nylon backboard would be used in order to prevent the electrical circuit from passing into any of the other parts of the sewing machine. It is also strong enough to have the wires attached but weak enough so the parts where the circuit needed to be threaded through could be cut.

Each component of the circuit board is made up of different metals as well as acids (in batteries), meaning that when there was no protection such as the rubber-coating or plastic cover, there was a high chance of something to happen when testing them out with a high voltage to make sure they would work properly.

Modern day Circuit Board

1980s Circuit Board

Date: 18/01/13   Candidate Name: April Elizabeth McCaffrey   Candidate Number: 3111

...precisely in a factory. Each component ...s work accurately. In the industrial ...ch is casted by the computer numerical ...re of the bit requires steel castings, ...components.

...ders because to different voltage and ...re not usually necessary in most

...es made by tools in order to suit the ...d alloys for specific uses or to provide ...Appropriate grooves, bevels, and holes are machined into the feet for their application. The finished presser foot is hand polished and plated with nickel.

When this is complete, the main framing of the sewing machine is created, using injection-moulded aluminium and highly powered cutting tools equipped with ceramic, carbide, or diamond-edged blades and are used to drill holes and to mill cuts and recesses to house features of the machine. The cover for the sewing machine are also precision-moulded to fit around and protect the machine's components.

Lastly, the circuit board is created. These are produced by high-speed robotics, then lay open to a burn-in period that is several hours long and are tested individually before being assembled in the machines.

Injection Moulding

Plastic pellets are placed in the hopper and into the screw. As this screw turns via the motor, the heaters melt these pellets into a liquid. This liquid is then pushed by the screw into the mould, where it would cool and become solid and shaped. This method was chosen over vacuum moulding because vacuum moulding had less flexibility in what could have been designed, even though it was a lot cheaper than injection moulding.

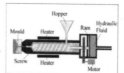

Each of these processes were specifically designed in order to maintain the lowest budget possibly needed for the creation of the sewing machine product, but it is also balanced out so it takes minimal time, cost and maximum quality and quantity. Modern robotics used in factories can keep time, quality, quantity and cost low as long as it works properly. It is also used in order to keep health and safety as high as possible; using machines will stop anything that is dangerous to humans to be used by people.

Date: 18/01/13   Candidate Name: April Elizabeth McCaffrey   Candidate Number: 3111

Modifying the design solution

1

This final section of the coursework requires you to compare the products against each other, stating in detail what exactly has changed in each development.

2

You then need to explain what you think the product will look like or be like in the future.

Modifying Design Solutions

The Sewing machine has changed in many ways since the 1940s, changing in almost every way except the finishing result. From the 1940s metal frame, and power, it changes into the 1980s PVC form along with motorised parts instead of a hand powered dial in order to get the needle to move. Having a hand dial made it much harder to control the fabric used, so when the 1940s had introduced a foot pedal, this problem was overcome as now you could use both hands to control. Even modern day sewing machines use a foot pedal, however, the foot pedal has been improved over the years in order to keep it durable for a consistent use. I think that the foot pedal will remain on future home sewing machines, but will continue to be improved in order to make it easier to store away (as there is no compartment in the sewing machine for the foot pedal) which would make it less likely to be broken by young children or accidental.

The foot pedal is used in order to control the movement of the needle, but the components of the mechanism has changed drastically over the years too. The hand dial meant that the needle could only move the speed of human movement, but when the motor was invented, the needle could move a lot faster, making it quicker to sew. In order to keep up with the faster movement, the gears used had to be changed from metal to nylon as nylon does not conduct heat as easily as metal would. This prevents over-heating the machine and breaking it. Although, nylon does need to be replaced after a few years as it wears down, so I think that future models of this product will contain a new material which works just as well, if not better, than nylon with a longer life range.

The needle of the 1940s was made of iron, and as mentioned before it brought a lot of problems with durability as it would break as soon as it rusted. Iron oxidation would not take too long with the needle bar as it was only a small piece, so it was easier for the oxygen to react. This problem was not solved in the 1980s, but only temporarily gradual. The needle would still need to be replaced, but in a year or so rather than the months it took to rust. In modern day sewing machines, they use stainless steel needle bars, which are prone to rust and scratches, meaning it would not break so easily, lasting many years. There wouldn't be another material found that could be better than the stainless steel as it does not have any type of disadvantage; it is not expensive, very durable and does the work needed without over-heating.

Date: 18/01/13   Candidate Name: April Elizabeth McCaffrey   Candidate Number: 3111

3

After you will need to look at each of your developments and detail any sustainability issues you can think of with each one. These are ways that the product damages the environment.

Sustainability issues

The 1940 sewing machine did not have many sustainability issues, but rather had a positive sustainability feedback. It did not break easily due to the heavy iron used for the frame and when it did break, it was very easy to fix again. This caused the product to be made less often with the added bonus that it did not pollute the earth when it did. However, due to the product first using electricity and newly found materials, it was extremely expensive and very hard to buy. Most sewing machines of this time had cost roughly the same amount as buying a car in the 1940s. It also didn't have many features so was quite hard to use.

The 1980s sewing machine was a huge leap from the 1940s, but the sustainability decreased terribly, causing more issues to be produced with each one made. Now that they were much cheaper to buy, more machines were created and more resources were used. This also caused pollution because of the new materials that were being used and because the older models were being thrown away even though they could still be used. This was for the simple reason that the latest models had many more features. The features, such as lighter weight, also caused the problem of the machines breaking easier since the 1980s were still trying to experiment with different ways to get a better result. The only positive sustainability was that it could do much better than the 1940s model, earning better results.

Lastly, the 2010 model had not changed too much from the 1980s. It was higher in price due to the economic issues of the country, but was still cheap enough for just about anyone to buy when they wanted to. The use of resources have been changed so they are recycled more, but pollution is still a sustainability issue even though science had reduced the amount of pollution through factories. Even more features have been added to this model, making it light weight still, but less likely to break than the 1980s model.

Date: 18/01/13   Candidate Name: April Elizabeth McCaffrey   Candidate Number: 3111

Bibliography

http://www.madehow.com/Volume-3/Sewing-Machine.html
http://sewing.about.com/od/sewingmachineparts/Sewing_Machine_Parts.htm
...ia.com

Don't forget to list all the websites or books you have used in your bibliography.

Coursework: 1B
Unit B231 *1B Manufacturing a Product*

For this piece of coursework you will be expected to design, make and test a product. Your teacher will give you all the details you need as OCR have a specific list of briefs that you can choose from.

Your product can be made in any area of DT from wood work to food technology or you can mix any of the areas together.

You will be marked on the following 5 areas:

Mark criteria

Section 1

provides a detailed and justified analysis of the client brief

produces and applies a justified design specification.

[7 8 9]

Section 2

develops a wide range of annotated design ideas considering:

- materials
- material constraints.

presents and justifies the selection of a design solution for the manufactured product.

[9 10 11 12]

Section 3

makes a complete, quality prototype of the design solution that allows for detailed testing.

[13 14 15 16 17 18]

Section 4

Selects and safely uses a wide range of appropriate materials, parts and components, processes, tools and equipment.

[7 8 9]

Section 5

suggests detailed and justified modifications to the design solution and original specification giving consideration to the use of modern materials, processes and technologies.

gives a detailed and justified explanation of how the product could be batch produced.

[9 10 11 12]

Section 1

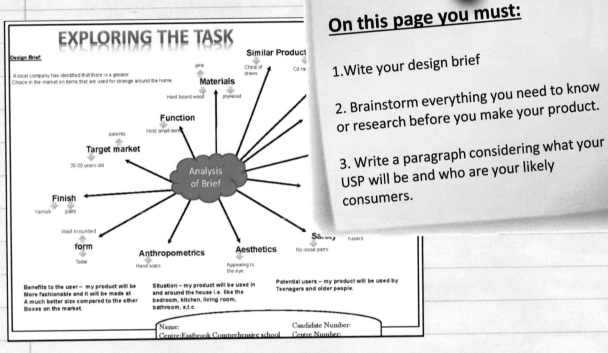

EXPLORING THE TASK

Design Brief:
A local company has identified that there is a greater
Choice in the market on items that are used for strange around the home.

Similar Product
- Chest of draws — pine
- Cd rac...

Materials
- Hard board wood
- plywood

Function
- Hold small item

Target market
- 20-30 years old
- parents

Finish
- Varnish
- paint
- Wall mounted

form
- Table

Analysis of Brief

Anthropometrics
- Hand sizes

Aesthetics
- Appealing to the eye

Safety
- No loose parts
- hazard

Benefits to the user – my product will be
More fashionable and it will be made at
A much better size compared to the other
Boxes on the market.

Situation – my product will be used in
and around the house i.e. like the
bedroom, kitchen, living room,
bathroom, e,t.c.

Potential users – my product will be used by
Teenagers and older people.

Name:
Centre:Eastbrook Comprehensive school

Candidate Number:
Centre Number:

On this page you must:

1. Wite your design brief

2. Brainstorm everything you need to know or research before you make your product.

3. Write a paragraph considering what your USP will be and who are your likely consumers.

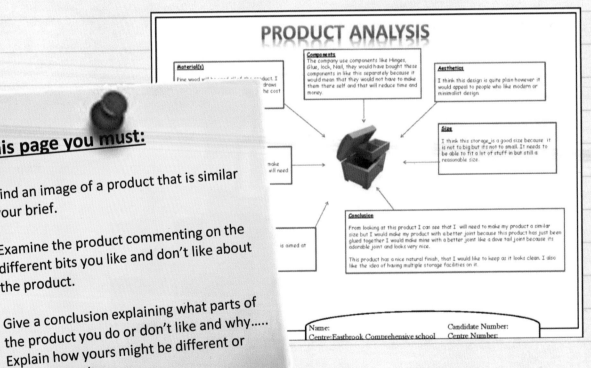

PRODUCT ANALYSIS

Material(s)
Pine wood will be used ...of the product. I ... draws ... he cost

Components
The company use components like Hinges,
Glue, lock, Nail, they would have bought these
components in like this separately because it
would mean that they would not have to make
them there self and that will reduce time and
money.

Aesthetics
I think this design is quite plain however it
would appeal to people who like modern or
minimalist design.

Size
I think this storage is a good size because it
is not to big but it's not to small. It needs to
be able to fit a lot of stuff in but still a
reasonable size.

...make
...will need

...is aimed at

Conclusion
From looking at this product I can see that I will need to make my product a similar
size but I would make my product with a better joint because this product has just been
glued together I would make mine with a better joint like a dove tail joint because its
adorable joint and looks very nice.

This product has a nice natural finish, that I would like to keep as it looks clean. I also
like the idea of having multiple storage facilities on it.

Name:
Centre:Eastbrook Comprehensive school

Candidate Number:
Centre Number:

On this page you must:

1. Find an image of a product that is similar your brief.

2. Examine the product commenting on the different bits you like and don't like about the product.

3. Give a conclusion explaining what parts of the product you do or don't like and why..... Explain how yours might be different or similar and why.

Section 1

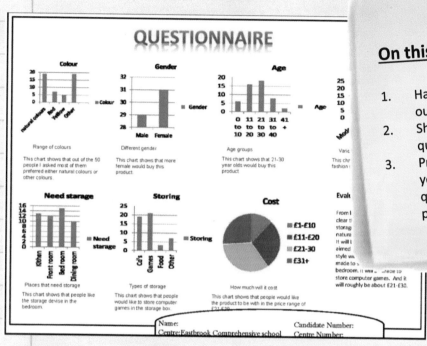

QUESTIONNAIRE

Colour

Range of colours

This chart shows that out of the 50 people I asked most of them preferred either natural colours or other colours.

Gender

Different gender

This chart shows that more female would buy this product.

Age

Age groups

This chart shows that 21-30 year olds would buy this product.

Need storage

Places that need storage

This chart shows that people like the storage devise in the bedroom.

Storing

Types of storage

This chart shows that people would like to store computer games in the storage box.

Cost

- £1-£10
- £11-£20
- £21-30
- £31+

How much will it cost

This chart shows that people would like the product to be with in the price range of £21-£30.

Name:
Centre:Eastbrook Comprehensive school

Candidate Number:
Centre Number:

On this page you must:

1. Have already written and carried out a questionnaire.
2. Show the results of your questionnaire in graph form.
3. Provide a conclusion stating what you have learnt from your questionnaire, or what your product will need to do.

SPECIFICATIONS

to store items in the bedrooms.

...otential the storage device will need to be big enough so

...n different storage components, for example drawers, or

...ge box that will be either natural colours or other colours ...e aimed at 21-30 year olds. The style will be fashion. It ...n the bedroom. It will be made to store computer ...+ about £21-£30.

...es of people, and be adaptable for different thing, ...ornaments for safe keeping.

...d be able to run your hand over it without ...good size, not too big or too small for all

Materials:

This storage box will be made from wood, because this is a good strong material and is easily repaired if damaged, and the target group have stated this is their most liked material.

Weight:

The weight of my product will be ideal weight so that it is light enough for some one to carry it.

Safety:

The Product can not have any sharp materials.
Not allowed to have any sharp corners
Nothing toxic
No loose or small parts

Cost Of Manufacture:

50% less than cost of retail

Manufacture:

Must be able to be made with CAD/CAM so it can be batch produced easily

Name:
Centre:Eastbrook Comprehensive school

Candidate Number:
Centre Number:

On this page you must:

1. You must write a list of things that your product must do or be like.

***To get good marks here you must explain why you have written each point by linking it to the results of your questionnaire.**

Section 2

GENERATING IDEAS FOR THEME

Evaluation

From my research on children jewellery box I found out they ... like they are a Disney character theme made and this has ins... similar to that my product. I will take the form of a popular fam...

Name:

On this page you must:

1. Fill the entire page with:
- Pictures
- Colours
- Words
- Shapes

That you might consider for your designs.

On this page you must:

1. Show at least 4 completely different ideas for a product that will meet your specifications.

** You will need to annotate them showing what materials you will use and how you might join some parts.

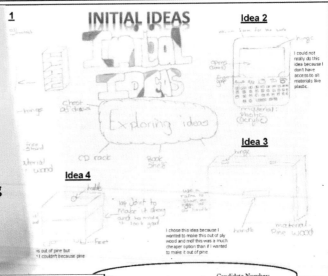

INITIAL IDEAS

Exploring ideas

Idea 2 — I could not really do this idea because I don't have access to all materials like plastic.

Idea 3

Idea 4

I chose this idea because I wanted to make this out of ply wood and mdf this was a much cheaper option than if I wanted to make it out of pine

Name: Centre:Eastbrook Comprehensive school   Candidate Number: Centre Number:

EVALUATION AGAINST SPECIFICATIONS

Function:
My product will be used to store items in the bedrooms.

Performance:
To be able to gain its full potential the storage device will need to be big enough so that it can store big items.
Must storage boxes contain different storage components, for example drawers, or individual sections.

Target Market:
From my research my storage box that will be either natural colours or other colours. It will be for females. It will be aimed at 21-30 year olds. The style will be fashion. It will be made to store things in the bedroom. It will be made to store computer games. And it will roughly be about £21-£30.

Aesthetics
My product must attract all types of people, and be adaptable for different thing, from storing jewellery to storing ornaments for safe keeping

Ergonomics:
It has to be smooth, you should be able to run your hand over it without harming yourself, it has to be a good size, not too big or too small for all purpose.

Materials:
This storage box will be made from wood, because this is a good strong material and is easily repaired if damaged, and the target group have stated this is their most liked material.

Weight:
The weight of my product will be ideal weight so that it is light enough for some one to carry it.

Safety:
The Product can not have any sharp materials
Not allowed to have any sharp corners.
Nothing toxic
No loose or small parts.

Cost Of Manufacture:
50% less than cost of retail.

Manufacture:
Must be able to be made with CAD/CAM so it can be batch produced easily

Idea 1
I really did like idea , but I could not use it because it did not reach all of my specifications. for example it did not meet the performance specification because it is not big enough to hold bigger items.
I couldn't do idea 1 because I do not have access to a metal bracket that I wanted to use to make it wall mountable.

Idea 2
I thought this idea was a very unusual idea. I would have used this idea but it didn't have all of my specifications like it didn't meet the material specification. because it wasn't made of wood so there for it would be much weaker if I was to make it out of plastic.
I could not really do this idea because I don't have access to all materials like plastic.

Idea 3 & Idea 4
In the end I decided to make idea 3 because it meets most of my specifications like it is made for the bedroom, it is a reasonable weight and it doesn't have any sharp corners or loose parts. it meets all of the specifications. I chose this idea because I wanted to make this out of ply wood and mdf this was a much cheaper option than if I wanted to make it out of pine
I nearly chose idea 4 but I preferred idea 3 just because it has got hinges I wanted to make this out of pine but because of the price I couldn't because pine is rather expensive

Name: Centre:Eastbrook Comprehensive school   Candidate Number: Centre Number:

On this page you must:

1. Evaluate each idea against your specifications.
2. Write a conclusion explaining in detail which idea you will develop more and why.

Section 2

MATERIAL RESEARCH

materials	Important properties	Material const
Plywood	Tough. Doesn't warp exterior plywood is water resistance.	Can split when cut.
Hardboard	Brittle. Goes soggy with water.	Tears easily difficult to finish
Medium density fireboard	Hard. Keeps edges well goes soggy with water.	Blunt tools shapes easily fini drills well.
chipboard	Brittle. Edges easily damaged.	Difficult to shape blunt tools poorly catches on drills.

I will be using plywood because it is available in large sheets, very strong, and it also reliable not to brake it is a b
has an almost natural look and feel to it that will appeal to a wider market.

Name:
Centre:Eastbrook Comprehensive scho

On this page you must:

1. Research **all** the possible materials that you **could** use to make your chosen idea.
2. Evaluate each material considering:
- What you might use it for.
- Cost of the material.
- Constraints or limitations of the material.

3. Make it obvious which materials you intend to use and why.

*You could do this as a table

On this page you must:

1. Show your final idea.
2. Annotate your design showing:
- How you will make or join parts.
- Identify parts that have changed from the initial idea and why.
- Identify the materials that will be used for each part.

DEVELOPMENT DRAWINGS

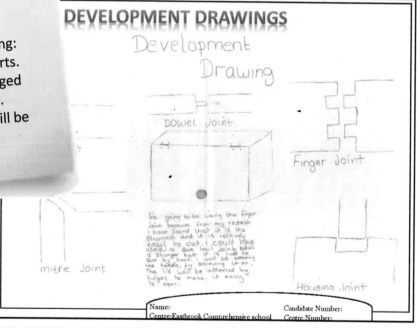

Development Drawing

Dowel Joint

Finger Joint

mitre Joint

Housing Joint

Name:
Centre:Eastbrook Comprehensive school
Candidate Number:
Centre Number:

Section 3

On this page you must:

1. Show pictures of your finished product from all different angles and close-ups of detailed work like hems, wood joints etc.

2. Annotate the different parts of your product explaining what the picture shows and brief explanation as to how you made it.

3. Explain how you could test your product to see if consumers would buy it and find flaws with the design.

FINISHED PRODUCT

This picture shows my finished box. It also shows that my box has been varnished so with varnish if there was any little marks you would be able to notice them and you clearly see that there is not.

This picture shows that my box opens using hinges it also shows that there is a large storage space inside for the user to use.

...picture shows that my product is made to an ...ellent standard. Also it shows that my product is in fully ...ng order and that it is completely finished

Name:
Centre:Eastbrook Comprehensive school

Candidate Number:
Centre Number:

TESTING

Questionnaire about my finished product

1. Do you think this product is suitable for its purpose?
2. Do you think this product is durable?
3. does this product look easy to use?
4. Does this product look light enough to carry?
5. Does this box look suitable for the bedroom?
6. Does this product look very appealable?

Answers about my finished product

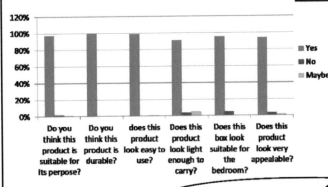

Name:
Centre:Eastbrook Comprehensive school

You could do an extra page for testing your product to help with your evaluation in section 5

EVIDENCE OF ME MAKING MY PRODUCT

In this picture it shows that the drawers were made very well and even the space that they go into were cut well.

In this picture I had just glued my box together. I learnt that you can cut the wood so that it is a bit to big and then after you can just sand paper it so that it is smooth and level.

In this picture it shows that both of my drawers work perfectly fine first of all the drawers did not slide in and out freely so all I had to do was adjust the thickness of the rail.

In this picture it shows that I am safely using the scroll saw. This picture also shows that I am using goggles and an apron.

In this picture it shows that I am nearly finished my box and that my drawers work correctly.

In this picture it shows that I have just hade to rail that will hold the draw and I also will place a sheet of mdf on to top this will be the base for the main section.

In this picture I had just filled in any little gaps and then sand papered it to improve the appearance.

In this picture it shows that I made a rail for my drawers so that it can easily slide. This was a very easy way of making a rail.

In this p...
am safe
sander
using m
my apro

Name:
Centre:Eastbrook Comprehensive school

On this section you must:

1. Show all the pictures of you making your product.
2. Explain what you are doing in each picture.

DIMENSION DRAWING

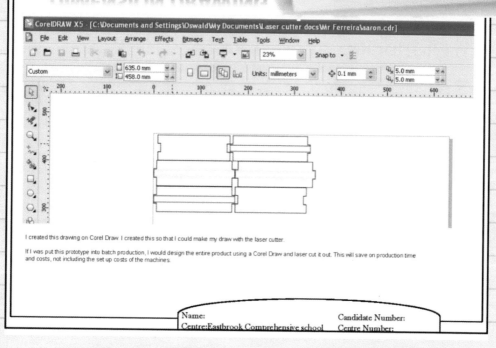

I created this drawing on Corel Draw. I created this so that I could make my draw with the laser cutter.

If I was put this prototype into batch production, I would design the entire product using a Corel Draw and laser cut it out. This will save on production time and costs, not including the set up costs of the machines.

Name:
Centre:Eastbrook Comprehensive school

Candidate Number:
Centre Number:

EVALUATION AGAINST SPECIFICATIONS

Specifications: Idea 3

Function:
My product will be used to store items in the bedrooms. ✓

Performance:
To be able to gain its full potential the storage device will need to be big enough so that it can store big items
Must storage [...] different [...] drawers, or

[...] for other colours. It will
[...] shion. It will be made
[...]rs. And it will roughly

[...]rent thing, from

[...] harming yourself, it

Materials:
This storage box will be made from wood, because this is a good strong material and is easily repaired if damaged, and the target group have stated this is their most liked material ✓

Weight:
The weight of my product will be ideal weight so that it is light enough for some one to carry it. ✓

Safety:
The Product can not have any sharp materials.
Not allowed to have any sharp corners.
Nothing toxic.
No loose or small parts. ✓

Cost Of Manufacture
50% less than cost of retail ✓

Manufacture
Must be able to be made with CAD/CAM so it can be batch produced easily ✗

[...] because it does contain multiple drawer compartments, as well as another storage place which will [...]tage because it was easy to make, and it is very strong and durable. If I was to make it again, I would [...] od

[...] about my product and about the finish I should use. The majority of them said that a natural colour [...] be females, this is because the majority of females would use this product the most. I know this [...]duct it would be stored mainly in the bedroom, as it has drawers, and a box to keep storage

[...] he space for the drawers were not perfect. The way I got around this was I created a bigger front for [...]d because it was not noticeable and made the presentation of my product a lot better, I think this

[...] specifications, however I am not certain if it is necessary for CAD/CAM to be used to ensure that [...] be changed to read 'must be suitable for batch production', as this is the ultimate goal.

Candidate Number:
[...]brook Comprehensive school   Centre Number:

On this page you must:

1. Copy your specifications from slide 6 and past them as a list here.
2. Look at your product and tick or cross each specification point if you think your product has or has not achieved it.
3. In the summary write a detailed evaluation explaining why your product did not meet the specification points you put a cross by and what you could change to meet them in future.
4. In the summary section you can also comment on any specifications that you wrote and now think are not useful or should be changed

You can not get full marks if you tick all of your specification points

---

BATCH PRODUCING THE PRODUCT

A production line will need to be set up, a production line is created to try and speed up the process of creating a product. using this method is a much better way of getting of producing my product because if I was to use machines to make the product it would be really expensive because the initial price off buying the machines.

Each worker is given one task to do and then they pass it down the production line to the next worker. This a good way off producing products because the worker will be very skilled at doing that one thing because they do that all day every day
The steps are:

1. Raw materials heat treated
2. Initial shaping and cutting
3. Grinding machine smooth's edges
4. Basic machine and processing
5. CNC machine accurately shapes the parts
6. The product is assembled by a machine operated buy a worker
7. Product quality checked and tested
8. Product passed on to packing department

I would employ ever semi skilled or unskilled workers operate the machines and this will keep the cost down

All of the workers must be able to switch from one part of the production line to another. They are called a "flexible workforce"

The production line can be changed at any time very quickly, so that different products can be made.

Sometimes individual parts of the product are bought from other companies and made on the production line

The production line runs for a certain amount of time and then they change the product

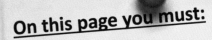

http://www.technology.st

Name:
Centre:Eastbrook Comprehensive school   Candi[...]   Centr[...]

On this page you must:

1. Research how your product might be made if you were going to make a bath of 100.
2. You must cover every step of the manufacturing process from design to making and testing.
3. There is always more than one way to do things so you must explain why you think the way you suggested is best.

Printed in Great Britain
by Amazon.co.uk, Ltd.,
Marston Gate.